Book 2

LANGUAGE SKILL BOOSTERS

George Moore

World Teachers Press®

Order Number 2-5108
ISBN 1-58324-030-6

C D E F 03 02

Educational Resources
395 Main Street
Rowley, MA 01969
www.worldteacherspress.com

Language Skill Boosters – Level 2

Language Skill Boosters is a series of seven books for elementary and middle school years. Each work sheet deals with a language skill specific to that year level, making it easy to link the content to what has been taught in the classroom. Each set of exercises is followed by a review sheet which checks the concepts, skills and content covered in the previous work. The review sheet may be done as a test or as review exercises with the student able to look back at previous work. A combination of these approaches could be used.

The basic work on each sheet is followed by a "Challenge" section which is more difficult. Most words can be found in the abridged dictionaries common in elementary and middle schools but a few words in these "Challenge" sections may need reference to a more comprehensive dictionary. Answers have been provided for your convenience.

Most exercises have brief answers so the work can be completed easily and quickly.

An individual student record sheet has been provided to communicate progress to parents.

Contents

page

Teachers Notes and Student Record 4-6

Rhyming Words 7

Following Directions 8

Phonics 9

Capital Letters and Periods 10

Opposites 11

Alphabet Search 12

Contractions 13

Plurals 14

Comprehension 15

Review 16

Phonics 17

Question Marks 18

Word Categories 19

Word Endings 20

Synonyms 21

Homophones 22

Report 23

Common Language Errors 24

Exclamation Points 25

Review 26

page

Plurals 27

Book Review 28

Nouns and Verbs 29

Word Categories 30

Opposites 31

Alphabetical Order 32

Rhyming Words 33

Syllables 34

Making Sentences 35

Review 36

Word Endings 37

Making Sentences 38

Sound Words 39

Compound Words 40

Common Language Errors 41

Homophones 42

Alphabetical Order 43

Plurals 44

Reading Comprehension 45

Review 46

Answers 47-48

Introduction

Consolidation and review activities are recognized as an integral part of learning and understanding a specific concept. Once a concept has been taught, students need several opportunities to practice, develop and understand the ideas and methods behind it.

Language Skill Boosters provides exactly this opportunity. The reinforcement of concepts through an assignment approach allows you to readily evaluate where each student may be having difficulties and provides parents with the opportunity to see how their child is achieving in the area of language.

The thirty-six assignments and four review sheets follow the same format, allowing the student to focus solely on the task at hand. This also develops a routine which aids the learning process and allows the student to attack independent activities/homework with confidence.

Strategies

Language Skill Boosters can be used as:

1. *Consolidation of classwork*
    Once a concept has been presented in class, the appropriate assignment can be photocopied and completed in class to consolidate and reinforce the concept.

2. *Review of classwork*
    At the end of a unit of work, the assignments can be used to assess the students' understanding of a particular concept. This allows you to focus further instruction at the point of need for individual students. This approach also provides a straightforward approach to evaluation and recording of the student's understanding of language.

3. *Homework activities*
    Each assignment can be photocopied and sent home for students to complete independently over the course of the week or pre-designated time period. Parents/Guardians can assist the student if they are having difficulties. The following approaches are encouraged:
    (a)   Assist the student with the process involved without solving the problem for the student, and
    (b)   encourage the student to try to solve the problem.
    Any problems encountered at home should be discussed with you at the earliest possible convenience. Each assignment focuses on one concept and the questions show a varying degree of difficulty.

Instructions

The instructions provided on each assignment are clear and concise. Each instruction has been carefully written to avoid ambiguity. This allows students to work as independently as they have no need to clarify the question.

Benefits

The benefits of *Language Skill Boosters* are many.

1. You can readily evaluate where each student is having success or difficulties.

2. Provides parents with the opportunity to observe how their child is achieving in the area of language.

3. Opens communication between school and home regarding each student's progress.

4. Opportunities are provided for students to practice, consolidate and review various concepts treated in class.

5. Students are able to take some responsibility for their own learning.

Conclusion

Language Skill Boosters is a useful tool for developing the knowledge and understanding of a broad range of language concepts. Students can develop a high level of confidence with the opportunities they are given to consolidate what they learn. This confidence leads to success and a positive self-image.

Page	Concept	Date	Comment	Signature
7.	Rhyming Words			
8.	Following Directions			
9.	Phonics			
10.	Capital Letters and Periods			
11.	Opposites			
12.	Alphabet Search			
13.	Contractions			
14.	Plurals			
15.	Comprehension			
16.	Review			
17.	Phonics			
18.	Question Marks			
19.	Word Categories			
20.	Word Endings			
21.	Synonyms			
22.	Homophones			
23.	Report			
24.	Common Language Errors			
25.	Exclamation Points			
26.	Review			
27.	Plurals			
28.	Book Review			
29.	Nouns and Verbs			
30.	Word Categories			
31.	Opposites			
32.	Alphabetical Order			
33.	Rhyming Words			
34.	Syllables			
35.	Making Sentences			
36.	Review			
37.	Word Endings			
38.	Making Sentences			
39.	Sound Words			
40.	Compound Words			
41.	Common Language Errors			
42.	Homophones			
43.	Alphabetical Order			
44.	Plurals			
45.	Reading Comprehension			
46.	Review			

1. Match the <u>rhyming</u> words.

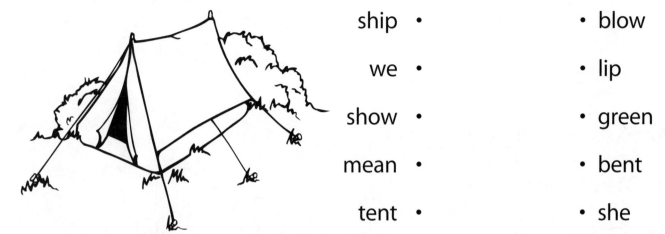

ship •   • blow

we •   • lip

show •   • green

mean •   • bent

tent •   • she

2. Draw a picture that <u>rhymes</u> with each of these words.

take   see   thin   sing

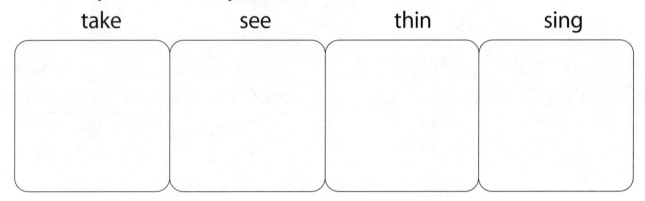

3. Circle all the words that <u>rhyme</u> with "cat."

bat   fat   pan

sit   that   mat

hat   pat

Challenge

1. Write three words that <u>rhyme</u> with these:

mad _____   _____   _____

now _____   _____   _____

Name: _____

1. Write yes or no.

(a) A duck can quack. _____

(b) Fish live in trees. _____

(c) A mouse can sing. _____

(d) A dog can wag its tail. _____

(e) Bats like to swim. _____

2. Finish the pictures.

The clown is holding four balloons. They are all different colors.

The dragon is green and yellow. Fire is coming out of its mouth.

Challenge

1. Color the fourth star orange.

   Color the second star blue.

   The other stars are purple.

Name: _____

1.   Add "ee" to these words. Draw and color the picture.

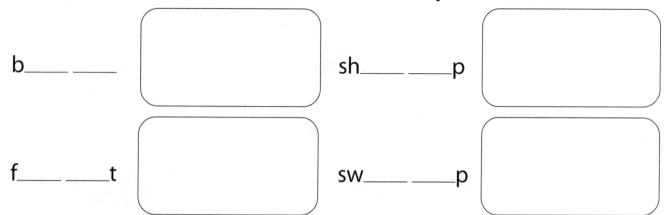

b____ ____

sh____ ____p

f____ ____t

sw____ ____p

2.   Color the icing on the cupcakes.

- **Color "oa" cupcakes pink.**
- **Color "ow" cupcakes purple.**

- **Color "ar" cupcakes brown.**
- **Color "ir" cupcakes yellow.**

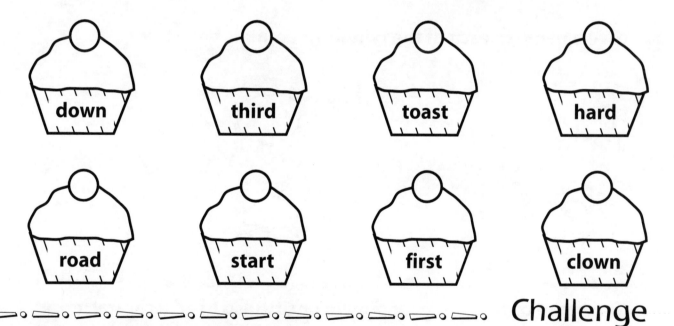

down   third   toast   hard

road   start   first   clown

Challenge

1.   Add "oo" or "ea" to these words.

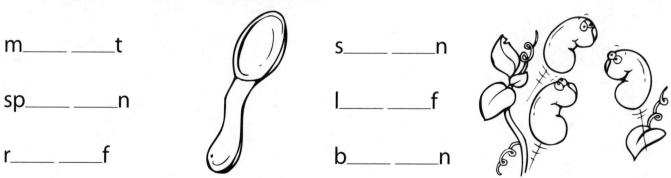

m____ ____t

s____ ____n

sp____ ____n

l____ ____f

r____ ____f

b____ ____n

Capital Letters and Periods

A sentence must begin with a <u>capital letter</u>.
A sentence must end with a <u>period</u>.

1. **Read each sentence. Circle the letters that should be capitals and put in the periods.**

   (a) we have a pond in our garden

   (b) two green frogs live in the pond

   (c) some tadpoles live in the pond too

   (d) soon there will be lots of frogs in our garden

   Capital letters are also used for the first letter of our <u>names</u>.

2. **Give a name to each of the people or animals below.**

Challenge

1. **The name of your street and town or city also need a capital letter. Write your name and address below.**

Name: _____

Day is the opposite of _night_.

1. Choose an opposite from the box to fit in the word shape.

| little | wet | clean | left | rich | slow |

poor

fast

big

dirty

right

dry

2. Write the opposite to finish the sentences.

hard   open   sunny

(a) Please (shut) _____ the door.

(b) It is a (cloudy) _____ day today.

(c) The problems were (easy) _____ to do.

Challenge

1. Write the opposites of these words.

sink _____   go _____

tall _____   laugh _____

Alphabet Search

1. Can you think of a food that <u>begins</u> with each letter of the alphabet?

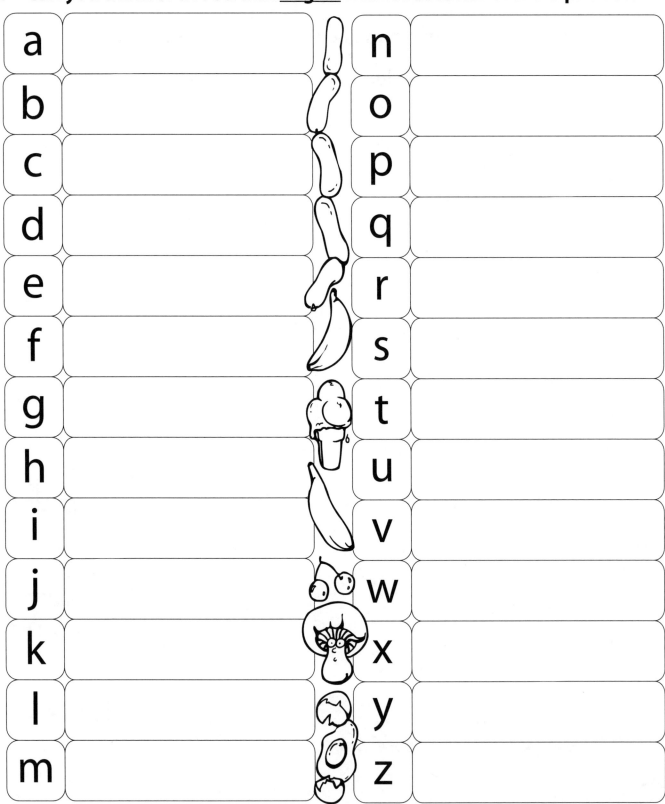

a		n	
b		o	
c		p	
d		q	
e		r	
f		s	
g		t	
h		u	
i		v	
j		w	
k		x	
l		y	
m		z	

Challenge

1. See if you can think of another food for each letter of the alphabet.

Contractions

We can make some words <u>shorter</u> by taking out letters.
An ' (apostrophe) is put in where letters have been left out.
For example, <u>can not</u> – <u>can't</u>

1.   Match the words with their contractions.

is not •   • he's

I am •   • I've

he is •   • wasn't

I have •   • isn't

was not •   • I'm

2.   Write the correct contraction.

we're	didn't	I'll	it's

did not = _____   it is   = _____

I will   = _____   we are = _____

Challenge

1.   Write the shortened word in the word shape.

they are

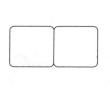

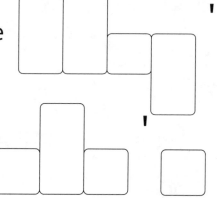

she is

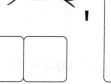

we will

When making words say more than one,
we usually add an "s".
For example, one cake – two cakes.

1.   Make these words more than one.

one bucket   two   _____

one spade   three _____

one shell   four   _____

Some words need "es" to say more than
one. For example, one box – two boxes.

2.   Make these words more than one.

one dish   two   _____

one glass   three _____

one peach   four   _____

one dress   five   _____

Challenge

1.   Add "s" or "es" to make these words more than one.

fox   _____   wish   _____

lunch _____   tent   _____

hand   _____   flower _____

beach _____   tiger _____

Comprehension

1.   Find six differences between the two pictures pictures above.

(a) _____

(b) _____

(c) _____

(d) _____

(e) _____

(f) _____

Challenge

1.   Read and draw.

(a)   Draw three balls on the ground.

(b)   Color the clown's shoes orange.

Review

1.   Color the words that rhyme with "sad."

| bad | pan | glad | pad | had | did |

2.   Write yes or no.

(a)   A cat can cook.   _____

(b)   Sharks have sharp teeth.   _____

(c)   Fish can laugh.   _____

(d)   Snakes have furry skin.   _____

3.   Add "oo" or "ow" to these words.

cl____ ____n

sp____ ____n

b____ ____k

cr____ ____d

4.   Write your full name.

My name is _____.

5.   Write a word that is opposite to fit in the word shape.

fast   shut   soft

6.   Add "s" or "es" to make these words say more than one.

box   _____

brush   _____

apple   _____

7.   Match the words.

we're •   • did not

we've •   • I will

I'll •   • we are

didn't •   • we have

Name: _____

1.   Read the sounds below.

| ir | ea | dr | ou | st |

| gr | ir | ee | oy | ow |

2.   Use the sounds to finish the words in the picture.

3.   Color the boxes when you have used the sound.

cl_____d

ne_____ _____

tr_____ _____

s_____ _____ t

b_____ _____ d

fl_____ _____ er

g_____ l

b_____ _____

_____ _____ ass

Challenge

1.   Circle the things in the picture which rhyme with these words.

word   crowd   enjoy   sea   feet

Name: _____

A sentence ends with a __question mark__ when it needs an answer.
For example, __What is your name?__

1. **Circle the question marks.**
   Write an answer and draw a picture.

   (a) What is your favorite food?

   _____

   (b) Who is your best friend?

   _____

2. **Put in a question mark or a period.**

   (a) How old are you ☐

   (b) The bin is next to the desk ☐

   (c) Can a frog fly ☐

   (d) Does an elephant have a trunk ☐

   (e) Please shut the door ☐

Challenge

1. **Write a sentence that needs a question mark.**
   Write an answer.

   _____

   _____

   Answer: _____

Name: _____

1.   Write the words below in their correct picture.

snail	orange	spoon	beetle
oven	pear	spider	peach
fridge	fly	banana	plate

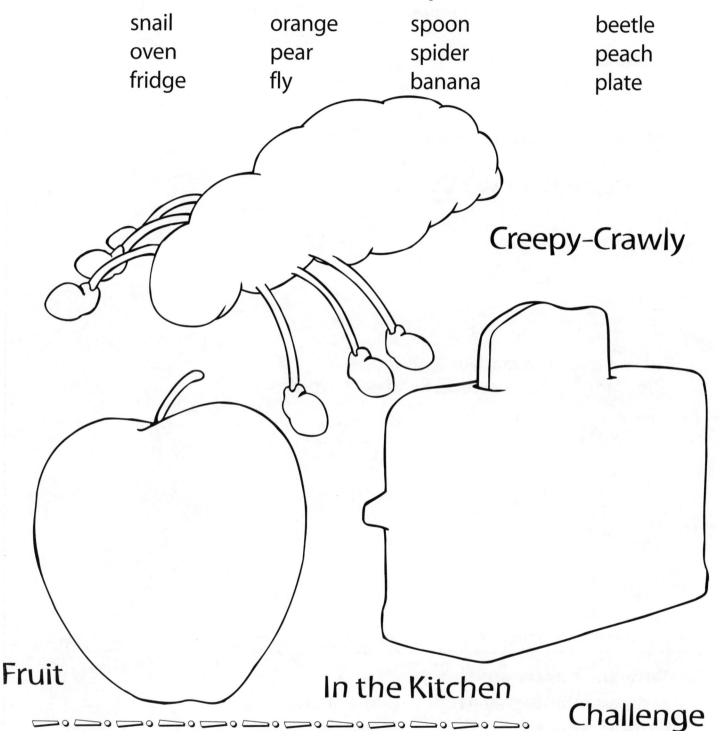

Creepy-Crawly

Fruit

In the Kitchen

Challenge

1.   Write two more words for each group.

red, yellow, _____, _____

three, seven, _____, _____

Name: _____

1.   Add "s" to these words. Read each word.

see _____   buy _____

draw _____   sleep _____

shout _____   hide _____

2.   Add "ed" to these words. Read each word.

jump _____   turn _____

look _____   ask _____

help _____   end _____

3.   Add "ing" to these words. Read each word.

sweep _____

teach _____

burn _____

spell _____

Challenge

1.   Write the correct word.

plays   played   playing

(a)   I _____ at my friend's house yesterday.

(b)   My brother _____ football and tennis.

(c)   We like _____ in our tree house.

Synonyms

***Fast* and *quick* are words that have nearly the same meaning.**

1.   Choose a similar word to finish the sentences.

tidy	mend	little	shut

(a)   A beetle is a (small) _____ insect.

(b)   Please (close) _____ the door.

(c)   My desk is very (neat) _____ .

(d)   Can you (fix) _____ the broken zipper?

2.   Circle the word which does not mean the same.

(a)
easy

simple

happy

(b)
laugh

yell

giggle

(c)
angry

mad

pretty

(d)
neat

dirty

messy

(e)
chair

bed

seat

(f)
talk

smile

grin

Challenge

1.   Unjumble these words to find a word with nearly the same meaning.

damp – t**we**   _____

high – a**t**ll   _____

speak – a**t**kl   _____

start – o**g**   _____

Name: _____

Sometimes words sound alike but have a different spelling.
For example, <u>son</u> and <u>sun</u>.

1. **Write the correct word in the space.**

(a) Did you see that (bear, bare) _____ at the zoo?

(b) My sister is (for, four) _____ years old.

(c) A pig has a curly (tail, tale) _____.

(d) Our dog dug a (hole, whole) _____ in the garden.

2. **Find these homophones in the word puzzle.**

t	l	p	h	e	a	r	w
o	k	e	k	n	o	w	i
o	e	a	t	q	c	o	t
m	r	r	p	a	i	r	c
f	e	w	r	d	n	o	h
w	h	i	c	h	t	w	o

witch   which

to   two   too

pear   pair

know   no

here   hear

Challenge

1. Unjumble these homophones.

(a) ese _____

     sae _____

(b) eb _____

     ebe _____

(c) wkee _____

     awke _____

(d) isal _____

     asle _____

**1.   Write a report about your pet or a pet you would like to own.
Fill in the information below.**

My pet is a _____.

This is a picture of my pet.

My pet's name is:

_____

The color of my pet is: _____

My pet is covered with: _____

My pet likes to: _____

_____

_____

Challenge

My pet lives:	My pet eats:

Common Language Errors

1. Read this sentence.

Me and my mom went shopping.

It should say...

My mom and I went shopping.

We should say the other people first and ourselves last. Also, when we speak about ourselves, we say "I."

2. Rewrite these sentences correctly.

(a) Me and my sister walk to school.

_____

_____

(b) Me and Dad like going to the beach.

_____

_____

Challenge

1. Color the correct word.

(a) I have | did | | done | my best work.

(b) Brett | was | | were | late for school.

(c) We | is | | are | moving to a new house.

(d) Do you | has | | have | a pet goldfish?

(e) My sister and | me | | I | will clean our bedroom.

Exclamation Points

*An **exclamation point** is used at the end of a group of words or a sentence when it needs to be said strongly. For example, **Look out!***

1. Circle the exclamation points. Color the pictures.

What a mess!

Watch out for the puddle!

2. Put in an exclamation point or a period.

(a) The cat sleeps on the mat ☐

(b) Come here at once ☐

(c) Fire ☐ Fire ☐

(d) Please put the book on the desk ☐

Challenge

1. Write a sentence that needs an exclamation point.

_____

2. Write a sentence that needs a period.

_____

1.   Put in a question mark or an exclamation point.

  (a)   Do you have a red car ☐

  (b)   Watch out for the car ☐

  (c)   Can you count to twenty ☐

2.   Circle the word which is different.

  (a) apple   peach   car   pear   **(b)** red   tree   blue   green

3.   Add "ed" to these words.

   jump _____   look _____

4.   Add "ing" to these words.

   sleep _____   draw _____

5.   Circle the word which is different.

   small   tidy   little   big   fast   quick

6.   Write the correct word in the space.

  (a)   Can you (here, hear) _____ the wind?

  (b)   There are seven days in one (week, weak) _____.

7.   Color the correct word.

  (a)   My Dad and me   I like going fishing.

  (b)   Her sister was   were late for school.

Name: _____

For many words ending in "y," change the "y" to "i" and add "es" to make them plural. For example, __baby__ – __babies__.

1. **Fill in the missing words.**

Singular	Plural
puppy	
party	
	stories
	ladies
baby	

2. **Draw pictures for the following words.**

puppies	lady	poppies

Challenge

1. **Put these words into sentences.**

stories _____

_____

story _____

_____

**1.   Brent Bookworm is looking for a good book to read.
Tell him about your latest reading adventure.**

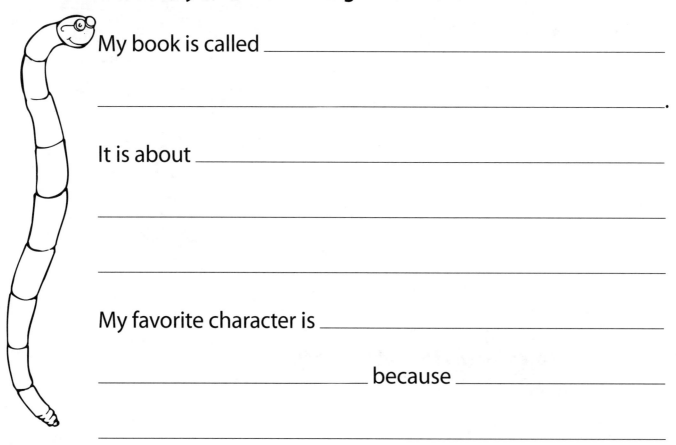

My book is called _____

_____.

It is about _____

_____

_____

My favorite character is _____

_____ because _____

_____

Challenge

1.   Draw your favorite character from the book.

Name:

__Nouns__ are naming words. __Verbs__ are doing words.
For example, __The cat is drinking milk__.
The __nouns__ in this sentence are: __cat__ and __milk__.
The __verb__ in this sentence is: __drinking__.

1.   Look at the picture below.

2.   List all the nouns you can see. _____

_____

_____

3.   List all the verbs you can see happening. _____

_____

_____

Challenge

1.   Write a sentence about something happening in the picture.
Underline the verbs and circle the nouns.

_____

_____

Word Categories

*The words you will use on this page are something to do with the **sea**.*
Have fun doing the activities!

1. **Find <u>little</u> words in these sea words.**
    For example, jellyfish – jelly, fish, is.

    sand _____

    beachball _____

    stingray _____

2. **Write the names of these sea creatures.**

    sea   fish   sword   snake   horse

    _____

    _____

    _____

3. **<u>Unjumble</u> these words. All of them are things you might take to the beach.**

    d**s**ape _____   ta**h** _____

    wel**to** _____   uc**b**ekt _____

Challenge

1. **Cross out every second letter. The letters left over will be something else you can take to the beach.**

    u n m o b p r b e k l d l r a

Name: _____

1. Match the opposites.

fast   black   far   good-bye
•   •   •   •

•   •   •   •
hello   slow   white   near

2. Find the opposite of these words in the puzzle.

walk   tall

young   high

full   remember

light   soft

bottom   laugh

e	m	p	t	y	f	k	o
r	d	o	h	l	o	w	l
u	a	d	a	u	r	o	d
n	r	c	r	y	g	t	y
b	k	g	d	r	e	o	m
l	s	h	o	r	t	p	f

3. Write the opposite to finish the sentences.

night   loud   front

(a) The music was very (soft) _____.

(b) Some animals hunt for food during the (day) _____.

(c) Please put the bag on the (back) _____ seat.

Challenge

1. Draw a picture for a pair of opposites on this page.

_____   _____

Name: _____

1.   Number these people who help us in <u>alphabetical order</u>.

farmer ( )   baker ( )   doctor ( )   pilot ( )

2.   Write these words in alphabetical order.

one   ten   eight   May   July   April

seven   four   September   October

_____   _____

_____   _____

_____   _____

_____   _____

_____   _____

Challenge

1.   Write two words that begin with each letter.

m _____   _____

r _____   _____

g _____   _____

Name: _____

1.   Write a rhyming word for each food.

peach _____   chips _____

cake _____   flour _____

cheese _____   toast _____

2.   Unjumble these words. All of them rhyme!

ntet _____   tewn _____

enst _____   ntde _____

stepn _____   netr _____

Challenge

1.   Find the words hidden in the Word Search

c	o	o	k	i	n	g	s	o	r
l	h	o	n	e	y	o	t	c	o
e	u	d	w	d	g	l	i	l	c
a	n	c	r	o	w	d	c	o	k

u	h	a	n	g	k	s	o	n	j	k	w	e
d	a	y	d	c	n	u	r	s	e	o	n	t
k	n	p	b	f	e	e	l	e	t	c	e	y
o	d	a	t	a	l	k	i	n	g	k	e	t

cooking	clean	hang	hand	hung
crowd	stick	day	clown	rocket
honey	gold	feel	talking	nurse door

Name: _____

Words can be broken into syllables to help us spell words.
For example, "under" has two syllables "un" and "der."

1.   Sort these words into one or two syllables.

apple   crayon   pen   desk   teacher   bin   door

tree   ruler   bird   table   pad   lemon   window

One Syllable	Two Syllables

Challenge

1.   Write the number of syllables after each word.

tiger ☐   sandal ☐   dress ☐

eagle ☐   elephant ☐   football ☐

ship ☐   banana ☐   umbrella ☐

Making Sentences

1.   Unjumble these sentences.

(a)   is It today. raining

_____

(b)   like cake. I chocolate

_____

(c)   fly. kite can A

_____

(d)   has ladybug A spots.

_____

2.   Write an ending to complete these sentences.

(a)   My favorite colors are _____

_____

(b)   She was late for school because _____

_____

(c)   A clown can _____

_____

Challenge

1.   Write a beginning to complete these sentences.

(a)   _____ has pretty colors on it.

(b)   _____ can hide in its shell.

Name: _____

1. **Make these words say more than one.**

   puppy _____ story _____

2. **Circle the nouns (naming words) in this sentence.**

   The dog is eating a bone.

3. **Circle the verb (doing word) in this sentence.**

   The dog is eating a bone.

4. **Find little words in these.**

   jellyfish _____

   beachball _____

5. **Match the opposites.**

   high •   • empty

   full •   • near

   hello •   • low

   far •   • good-bye

6. **Write a rhyming word.**

   trick _____

   floor _____

   away _____

7. **Write these words in alphabetical order.**

   ship   truck   car   van

   _____

8. **Color the words with two syllables.**

   lemon   bird   dress   teacher   ruler

Name: _____

1.   Add "<u>ed</u>" and "<u>ing</u>" to these words. Read each word.

match   _____   _____

play   _____   _____

burn   _____   _____

help   _____   _____

2.   Add "<u>ed</u>" and "<u>ing</u>" to these words. Read each word. This time you will need to double the last letter. For example, hop – hopping.

hop _____   _____

chop _____   _____

stop _____   _____

jog _____   _____

skip _____   _____

Challenge

1.   Add "<u>ed</u>" and "<u>ing</u>" to these words. Read each word. This time you will need to drop the final "<u>e</u>." For example, tast<u>e</u>, tast<u>ed</u>, tast<u>ing</u>.

bounce _____   _____

hope   _____   _____

bake   _____   _____

smile _____   _____

Making Sentences

1. **Cut and paste the words at the bottom of the page to make sentences about farm animals.**

Describing Words (adjectives)	Farm Animals (nouns)	Action (verbs)
	lambs	
	ducks	
	cows	
	chickens	
	horses	
	kittens	

Challenge

1. **On a piece of paper write your own sentence about a farm animal.**

Hungry	sleep in a basket.
Noisy	peck at seeds.
Cute	say Quack! Quack!
Fat	gallop very fast.
Woolly	eat green grass.
Black	play in the field.

Sound Words

Some words sound like what they are describing. For example, tinkle.

1. **Draw a line to match the sound words to the correct picture.**

(a) splash •

(b) pop •

(c) swoosh •

(d) patter •

(e) bang •

(f) rustle •

(g) boom •

(h) tick •

(i) buzz •

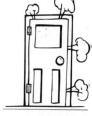

Challenge

1. **Write words to describe these sounds.**

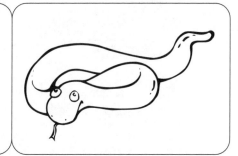

_____   _____   _____

Compound Words

Sometimes when we add two words together
we can make a new word.
For example, quick + sand = quicksand

1.   Fill in the missing words.

(a) _____air_____ + _____port_____ = _____

(b) _____ + _____room_____ = _____bedroom_____

(c) _____sun_____ + _____ = _____sunscreen_____

(d) _____sea_____ + _____shore_____ = _____

(e) _____ + _____day_____ = _____Sunday_____

(f) _____hand_____ + _____ = _____handstand_____

(g) _____broom_____ + _____stick_____ = _____

(h) _____ + _____ball_____ = _____football_____

(i) _____tooth_____ + _____ = _____toothache_____

Challenge

1.   Write two words that make up these compound words.

_____ + _____ = handshake

_____ + _____ = rainbow

_____ + _____ = staircase

_____ + _____ = doorknob

Common Language Errors

We use <u>an</u> before words starting with vowels.
For example, <u>an apple</u>.

1.   Write the five vowels here.

☐ ☐ ☐ ☐ ☐

2.   Write *"an"* or *"a"* and draw pictures for each one.

_____ elephant   _____ snake   _____ owl

_____ octopus   _____ zebra   _____ lizard

Challenge

1.   Write the first letter for these sea animals.

(a) an ☐yster   **(c)** a ☐ish   **(e)** a ☐rab

(b) a ☐ellyfish   **(d)** an ☐el   **(f)** a ☐hark

Name:_____

Homophones _are words which sound the same_
but have different spellings.
For example, <u>sea</u> _and_ <u>see</u>.

1.   **Match the words which have the same sound.**
     Choose a pair and draw a picture of each word.

by •	• eight
meet •	• meat
whole •	• hole
ate •	• buy

2.   **Color the correct word in the sentence.**

(a)   The wind | blue | | blew | the door shut.

(b)   I will | write | | right | a letter to my friend.

(c)   It was a wet and windy | knight | | night |.

(d)   Where is my teddy | bear | | bare | ?

Challenge

1.   **Put each homophone into a sentence to show its different meanings.**

(a) one _____

_____

(b) won _____

_____

Name: _____

1. Write the missing letters in the spaces.

(a) **a** comes before _____

(b) **f** comes after _____

(c) **k** comes between _____ and _____

(d) **l** comes before _____

(e) **o** comes between _____ and _____

(f) **z** comes after _____

2. Number these words in alphabetical order.

(a) ☐ elephant   ☐ tiger   ☐ bear

(b) ☐ beetle   ☐ ant   ☐ fly

(c) ☐ kitten   ☐ puppy   ☐ lamb

Challenge

1. Write these words in alphabetical order.

run   jump   skip   walk   leap   hop

_____

_____

Name: _____

When making words say more than one we usually add an "s."
For example, one rabbit – five rabbits.
Some words change when made plural.
For example, man – men.

1.   Write the plural for these.

foot

tooth

child

mouse

Some words don't change at all when made plural.
For example, one sheep – many sheep.

2.   Write the correct word.

sheep   deer   fish

(a) Andy caught one _____ yesterday.

(b) I saw a _____ on the lawn.

(c) This sweater is made from the wool of many _____.

Challenge

The words below say more than one. Write a word to make them single.

three birds – one _____   six chairs – one _____

two fish – one _____   three teeth – one _____

Read the story and answer the questions below.

A Visit to the Lake

On Sunday Sarah and Danny went to the lake. There were lots of shady trees there. They saw four ducks and two swans swimming in the lake.

Danny sailed his toy boat on the lake. It was red with white sails. Sarah played on the swing under a shady tree.

1. What day did Sarah and Danny go to the lake? _____

2. **Color yes or no.**

(a) The children saw four ducks.   yes   no

(b) Danny's boat was green and white.   yes   no

(c) Sarah played on a slide.   yes   no

3. How many swans were on the lake? _____

Challenge

1. **Circle the things that were at the lake.**

trees   house   ducks   boat

ball   swing   dog

2. **What do you think the weather was like at the lake?** _____

Name: _____

1. **Add _"ed"_ and _"ing"_ to these words.**

jog _____ _____

hop _____ _____

2. **Draw a picture to describe these sounds.**

bang   splash

3. **Join these words to make a new word.**

bed + room = _____

rain + bow = _____

foot + ball = _____

4. **Color the correct word.**

(a) I have | a | | an | apple in my lunch bag.

(b) We saw | a | | an | tadpole in the pond.

5. **Write the correct word in the space.**

(a) Would you like roast (meet, meat) _____ for dinner?

(b) My brother is (ate, eight) _____-years-old.

6. **Write the plural for these.**

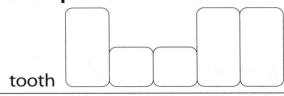

tooth   mouse

Answers

page 7 Rhyming Words

1. ship – lip, we – she, show – blow, mean – green, tent – bent
2. Teacher check
3. bat, fat, that, mat, hat, pat

Challenge

1. Teacher check

page 8 Following Directions

1. (a) yes (b) no (c) no (d) yes (e) no
2. Teacher check

Challenge

1. Teacher check

page 9 Phonics

Teacher check

Challenge

1. Teacher check

page 10 Capital Letters and Periods

Teacher check

page 11 Opposites

1. poor – rich, big – little, right – left, fast – slow, dirty – clean, dry – wet
2. (a) open (b) sunny (c) hard

Challenge

1. sink – float, tall – short, go – stop, laugh – cry

page 12 Alphabet Search

Teacher check

page 13 Contractions

1. is not – isn't, I am – I'm, he is – he's, I have – I've, was not – wasn't
2. didn't, it's, I'll, we're

Challenge

they are – they're, she is – she's, we will – we'll

page 14 Plurals

1. one bucket – two buckets, one spade – three spades, one shell – four shells
2. one dish – two dishes, one glass – three glasses, one peach – four peaches, one dress – five dresses

Challenge

foxes, lunches, hands, beaches, wishes, tents, flowers, tigers

page 15 Comprehension

(a) Three balls missing
(b) Spots on female clown's hat missing
(c) Button on female clown missing
(d) Crosses on male clown's buttons missing
(e) Fence tops are different
(f) Stripes on pants of male clown are missing

Challenge

1. Teacher check

page 16 Review

1. bad, glad, pad, had
2. (a) no (b) yes (c) no (d) no
3. clown, spoon, book, crowd
4. Teacher check
5. slow – fast, open – shut, hard – soft
6. boxes, brushes, apples
7. we're – we are, we've – we have, I'll – I will, didn't – did not

page 17 Phonics

Teacher check

Challenge

1. word – bird, crowd – cloud, enjoy – boy, sea – tree, feet – seat

page 18 Question Marks

1. Teacher check
2. a, c and d – question marks b and e – periods

Challenge

1. Teacher check

page 19 Word Categories

Creepy - Crawly – snail, beetle, spider, fly
Fruit – orange, pear, peach, banana
In the Kitchen – spoon, oven, fridge, plate

Challenge

1. Teacher check

page 20 Word Endings

Teacher check

Challenge

1. (a) played (b) plays (c) playing

page 21 Synonyms

1. (a) little (b) shut (c) tidy (d) mend
2. (a) happy (b) yell (c) pretty (d) neat (e) bed (f) talk

Challenge

1. damp – wet, speak – talk, high – tall, start – go

page 22 Homophones

1. (a) been (b) four (c) tail (d) hole
2.

Challenge

1. see – sea, be – bee, week – weak, sail – sale

page 23 Report

Teacher check

Challenge

1. Teacher check

page 24 Common Language Areas

(a) My sister and I walk to school.
(b) Dad and I like going to the beach.

Challenge

(a) done (b) was (c) are (d) have (e) I

page 25 Exclamation Points

1. Teacher check
2. (a) and (d) – periods
   (b) and (c) – exclamation points

Challenge

1. Teacher check

page 26 Review

1. (a) ? (b) ! (c) ?
2. (a) car (b) tree
3. jumped, looked
4. sleeping, drawing
5. (a) tidy (b) big
6. (a) hear (b) week
7. (a) I (b) was

page 27 Plurals

1. puppy – puppies, party – parties, story – stories, lady – ladies, baby – babies
2. Teacher check

Challenge

1. Teacher check

Answers

page 28 Book Review
Teacher check

page 29 Nouns and Verbs
Teacher check

page 30 Word Categories
1. sand – and, an, a
   beachball – beach, each, ball, all, be, a
   stingray – sting, ray, tin, in, a
2. seahorse, swordfish, sea snake
3. spade, hat, towel, bucket

Challenge
1. umbrella

page 31 Opposites
1. fast – slow, black – white, far – near,
   good-bye – hello
2.

3. (a) loud   (b) night   (c) front

Challenge
Teacher check

page 32 Alphabetical Order
1. baker, doctor, farmer, pilot
2. eight, four, one, seven, ten
   April, July, May, October, September

Challenge
1. Teacher check

page 33 Rhyming Words
1. Teacher check
2. ntet – tent, enst – sent, stepn – spent,
   tewn – went, ntde – dent, netr – rent

page 34 Syllables
one syllable – door, pen, desk, bin, tree,
bird, pad

two syllables – apple, crayon, teacher, ruler,
lemon, window, table

Challenge
1. one syllable – dress, ship
   two syllables – tiger, sandal, eagle, football
   three syllables – elephant, banana,
   umbrella

page 35 Making Sentences
1. (a) It is raining today.
   (b) I like chocolate cake. (c) A kite can fly.
   (d) A ladybug has spots.
2. Teacher check

Challenge
1. Teacher check

page 36 Review
1. puppy – puppies, story – stories
2. dog, bone
3. eating
4. jellyfish – jelly, fish, is, l,
   beachball – beach, each, a, ball, all, be
5. high – low, full – empty, hello – good-bye,
   far – near
6. Teacher check
7. car, ship, truck, van
8. lemon, teacher, ruler

page 37 Word Endings
1. matched , matching; played, playing;
   burned, burning; helped, helping
2. hopped, hopping; chopped, chopping;
   stopped, stopping; jogged, jogging;
   skipped, skipping

Challenge
bounced – bouncing, hoped – hoping,
baked – baking, smiled – smiling

page 38 Making Sentences
Teacher check

Challenge
1. Teacher check

page 39 Sound Words
1. (a) splash – fish (b) pop – cork
   (c) swoosh – bird (d) patter – rain
   (e) bang – door (f) rustle – leaves
   (g) boom – drum (h) tick – clock
   (i) buzz – bee

Challenge
1. Teacher check

page 40 Compound Words
Teacher check

page 41 Common Language Errors
1. a, e, i, o and u
2. an elephant, a snake, an owl, an octopus, a
   zebra, a lizard

Challenge
(a) an oyster (b) a jellyfish (c) a fish
(d) an eel   (e) a crab   (f) a shark

page 42 Homophones
1. by - buy, meet - meat, whole - hole,
   ate - eight
2. (a) blew (b) write (c) night (d) bear

Challenge
1. Teacher check

page 43 Alphabetical Order
1. (a) b   (b) e   (c) j and l   (d) m
   (e) n and p   (f) y
2. (a) bear, elephant, tiger
   (b) ant, beetle, fly
   (c) kitten, lamb, puppy

Challenge
1. hop, jump, leap, run, skip, walk

page 44 Plurals
1. foot – feet, child – children, tooth – teeth,
   mouse – mice
2. (a) fish   (b) deer   (c) sheep

Challenge
1. one bird, one fish, one chair, one tooth

page 45 Reading Comprehension
1. Sunday
2. (a) yes   (b) no   (c) no
3. two

Challenge
1. trees, ducks, boat, swing
2. Teacher check

page 46 Review
1. jogged - jogging, hopped - hopping
2. Teacher check
3. bedroom, rainbow, football
4. (a) an   (b) a
5. (a) meat   (b) eight
6. teeth, mice

World Teachers Press®